ENDANGERED PANDAS

John Crossingham & Bobbie Kalman

Crabtree Publishing Company

www.crabtreebooks.com

Earth's Endangered Animals Series
A Bobbie Kalman Book

Dedicated by Kathy Middleton
For my niece Genevieve Wilson, my favorite animal

Editor-in-Chief
Bobbie Kalman

Writing team
John Crossingham
Bobbie Kalman

Substantive editor
Kelley MacAulay

Project editor
Kristina Lundblad

Editors
Molly Aloian
Robin Johnson
Rebecca Sjonger
Kathryn Smithyman

Design
Margaret Amy Reiach

Cover design and series logo
Samantha Crabtree

Production coordinator
Katherine Kantor

Photo research
Crystal Foxton

Consultant
Patricia Loesche, Ph.D., Animal Behavior Program,
Department of Psychology, University of Washington

Illustrations
Barbara Bedell: page 7
Margaret Amy Reiach: title, pages 5, 11 (bottom)
Bonna Rouse: back cover, pages 11 (top), 13, 22

Photographs
Bruce Coleman Inc.: Tom Brakefield: page 27 (top);
 Fritz Polking: page 9 (top);
 Lynn M. Stone: pages 25 (right), 30
Minden Pictures: Gerry Ellis: pages 12, 17, 24, 25 (left), 27 (bottom), 29;
 Katherine Feng/Globio: page 14;
 Konrad Wothe: page 8
Pete Oxford/naturepl.com: page 15
Andy Rouse/NHPA: page 9 (bottom)
Visuals Unlimited: Bill Kamin: page 10;
 Fritz Polking: pages 7, 19, 22-23
Erwin & Peggy Bauer/Wildstock: pages 3, 18, 20
©Wolfgang Kaehler, www.wkaehlerphoto.com: pages 16, 28
Other images by Corel, Creatas, and Digital Stock

Crabtree Publishing Company

www.crabtreebooks.com   1-800-387-7650

Copyright © 2005 CRABTREE PUBLISHING COMPANY.
All rights reserved. No part of this publication may be
reproduced, stored in a retrieval system or be transmitted in
any form or by any means, electronic, mechanical, photocopying,
recording, or otherwise, without the prior written permission
of Crabtree Publishing Company. In Canada: We acknowledge the
financial support of the Government of Canada through the Book
Publishing Industry Development Program (BPIDP) for our
publishing activities.

Cataloging-in-Publication Data
Crossingham, John.
 Endangered pandas / John Crossingham & Bobbie Kalman.
  p. cm. -- (Earth's endangered animals series)
 Includes index.
 ISBN-13: 978-0-7787-1858-1 (RLB)
 ISBN-10: 0-7787-1858-1 (RLB)
 ISBN-13: 978-0-7787-1904-5 (pbk.)
 ISBN-10: 0-7787-1904-9 (pbk.)
 1. Pandas--Juvenile literature. 2. Endangered species--Juvenile literature.
I. Kalman, Bobbie. II. Title.
 QL737.C214C77 2005
 599.789'168--dc22   2005000347
                                              LC

**Published in
the United States**
PMB16A
350 Fifth Ave.
Suite 3308
New York, NY
10118

**Published
in Canada**
616 Welland Ave.,
St. Catharines, Ontario
Canada
L2M 5V6

**Published in the
United Kingdom**
73 Lime Walk
Headington
Oxford
OX3 7AD
United Kingdom

**Published
in Australia**
386 Mt. Alexander Rd.,
Ascot Vale (Melbourne)
VIC 3032

Contents

Endangered pandas 4

What are pandas? 6

Where do pandas live? 8

Big, furry bodies 10

A panda's life cycle 12

Life with Mom 14

Panda behavior 16

Bamboo eaters 18

Losing their habitats 20

Poaching pandas 22

Not enough cubs 24

Protecting pandas 26

Pandemonium! 28

Help a panda! 30

Glossary and Index 32

Endangered pandas

The giant panda is probably the world's most famous **endangered** animal! In the past, giant pandas were common in the **wild**, or the natural places not controlled by people. Today, there are only about 1,600 giant pandas living in the wild.

WWF, *which stands for World Wildlife Fund, is an organization that works to protect animals and the wild places where they live. In 1961, WWF chose the giant panda as its **logo**. The image of a panda now reminds people to help all animals.*

Giant pandas are often known simply as "pandas."

Words to know

Scientists use certain words to describe animals in danger. Some of these words are listed below.

vulnerable Describes animals that may soon become endangered

endangered Describes animals that are at risk of dying out in the wild

critically endangered Describes animals that are at high risk of dying out in the wild

extinct Describes animals that are no longer living anywhere on Earth or animals that have not been seen alive for at least 50 years

What are pandas?

Giant pandas are **mammals**. Mammals are **warm-blooded** animals. The body temperatures of warm-blooded animals stay about the same in hot or cold weather. Mammals have **backbones**, and most are covered with fur or hair. Giant pandas have black-and-white fur. Young mammals drink milk from the bodies of their mothers.

Alone in the forest

Pandas are **solitary** animals, which means they usually live alone. Since pandas do not live in groups, it is hard for scientists to count them. Pandas are also hard to count because they live in thick forests, where they can easily hide.

Giant pandas are large, strong animals, but they are also gentle and shy.

6

Panda relatives

There are two kinds of pandas—giant pandas and red pandas. The word "panda" means "bamboo-eater." Both giant pandas and red pandas eat bamboo, but these two animals are probably not close relatives. Giant pandas seem to be more closely related to bears. Red pandas seem to be more closely related to raccoons. This book is about giant pandas.

This giant panda is eating bamboo.

Red pandas

Red pandas look very different from giant pandas. Red pandas are similar in size to raccoons. They live in parts of China, Nepal, and India. Red pandas are also endangered animals.

Where do pandas live?

Most panda habitats are in the southwestern part of China. Many pandas live in a province called Sichuan.

Pandas live in forests that grow high in the **mountainous** areas of China. Mountain forests are the panda's **habitat**, or the natural place where the panda lives. This habitat is perfect for the panda because it is cool and damp and contains a lot of fresh water. It also has plenty of bamboo, which is the panda's favorite food.

High, high up

There are many kinds of bamboo, but pandas eat only the kinds that grow high up on mountains. Pandas move down from the mountains during winter because the temperature is warmer near the bottom of the mountains.

Home on the range

Each panda lives alone in a **home range**, or territory. A male panda's home range is usually six to seven square miles (15.5 to 18 sq km). A female panda's home range is usually four to five square miles (10 to 13 sq km). Pandas do not live in open spaces. They choose home ranges in the thick forests that are found on steep mountainsides.

Pandas are excellent climbers. They often climb trees to take long naps.

Taking a rest

Most pandas find **dens**, or shelters, within their home ranges. Pandas often use caves or hollow trees as dens. The hollow tree on the right is a panda den. Pandas use their dens when they need resting places. Some pandas rest in their dens every day, whereas others do not. Most pandas use their dens for a while and then find new homes.

Big, furry bodies

Adult pandas have large, strong bodies. Their bodies are covered in thick, oily, black-and-white fur. This fur keeps a panda warm in two ways. First, thick fur holds in the panda's body heat. Second, the oil in the fur keeps water away from the panda's skin. Dry skin stays warmer than wet skin does.

How big?

Adult pandas are usually five feet (1.5 m) long. Female pandas weigh about 200 pounds (91 kg), whereas male pandas weigh about 220 pounds (100 kg).

Pandas have long, sharp claws. They use their claws to climb trees.

On the move

Pandas move around on all four legs. They shuffle and sway when they walk. As pandas walk, their **forepaws**, or front paws, point inward. Pandas move slowly most of the time. They run only when they are in danger.

Pandas have strong cheek muscles and large teeth that help them break apart pieces of bamboo.

A panda has a white head with black ears and eye patches.

*Pandas have strong **hind legs**, or back legs. They stand on their hind legs to reach food that is high off the ground.*

"Thumbs" up!

Forepaws allow a panda to hold bamboo. Each forepaw has five toes and a large bone on the wrist that looks like a thumb. A panda uses its toes and false thumb to grip bamboo tightly as it chews the tough plants.

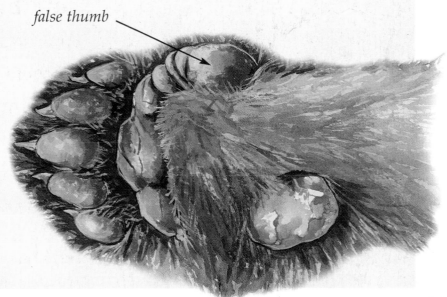

false thumb

11

A panda's life cycle

As an animal grows, it goes through a series of changes called a **life cycle**. A mammal's life cycle begins when the animal is born. The mammal grows and changes until it is **mature**, or an adult. A mature mammal can **mate**, or join together with another mammal of the same kind to make babies.

WWF scientists believe that most pandas live for ten to fifteen years in the wild.

Growing up

Before it is born, a panda grows inside its mother's body for about four-and-a-half to five months. A mother panda gives birth to one or two **cubs**, or baby pandas. When a mother gives birth to two cubs, she often cares for only one. The other cub usually dies. A newborn cub is tiny, blind, and helpless. Its eyes do not open until the cub is between six and eight weeks old. The cub **nurses**, or drinks milk from its mother's body. It nurses for eight to nine months, but it stays with its mother until it is about two years old. The cub then leaves its mother to live on its own. When the panda is mature, it is ready to have babies of its own.

Pandas are mature when they are five or six years old. Mature pandas can mate.

A newborn cub is pink, with thin, white fur. It weighs only 0.25 pounds (0.1 kg). The cub grows quickly over the next two months.

At about five to eight months of age, the cub begins to live outside the den, among the trees. The cub gradually stops nursing and starts eating bamboo.

When it is three to four months old, the cub begins to walk. It weighs about fifteen pounds (6.8 kg), and its fur has grown in. The cub usually stays inside its mother's den.

13

Life with Mom

A newborn panda makes noises to let its mother know when it is hungry or in trouble.

For many months after it is born, a cub needs its mother to feed it and to keep it warm. The cub also needs its mother to protect it from **predators**. Predators are animals that hunt and kill other animals for food.

Life in the den

A mother panda raises her cub inside her den. For the first few weeks of the cub's life, the mother does not leave the den. She does not even leave to eat bamboo! During this time, the mother lives off the food energy stored in her body fat.

Side by side

When a cub is about three weeks old, its black-and-white fur begins to grow in. The cub looks like its mother, but it is much smaller. The mother panda now takes her cub along with her when she goes into the forest to feed.

The mother panda hides her cub in a thick bamboo patch while she eats. When the cub is about five months old, it starts climbing trees. In the trees, the cub can play, sleep, and hide from predators. It learns how to survive by watching its mother.

A panda cub learns how to eat bamboo by watching its mother.

Panda behavior

When it is about two years old, a panda leaves its mother to find its own home range. It makes **scent markings** to keep other pandas out of its territory. Each panda has **scent glands** on its bottom. To leave scent markings, a panda rubs its bottom against rocks and trees in its home range, as shown left. The scent warns other pandas to stay out of the area!

Changing scents

The only time a panda looks for other pandas is when it is ready to mate. During this time, a female panda's scent changes. Her new scent lets male pandas know that she is ready to mate.

16

Eating through bamboo

A panda begins eating a **stalk** of bamboo by gripping the stalk with its forepaws. The panda strips off the leaves before it eats them. It then grinds up the stalk with its **molars**, or back teeth. The part of the bamboo that a panda needs the most is the **pith** inside the stalk. The pith is sweet and contains most of the plant's nutrients.

Pandas need a lot of water every day. If the bamboo they are eating is too dry, pandas look for water to drink in mountain streams or rivers.

Losing their habitats

*When trees are clear-cut from steep mountain slopes, **landslides** can sweep away large areas of bamboo.*

The greatest threat to pandas is **habitat loss**. Habitat loss is the destruction of wild areas where animals live. When bamboo forests are cut down, pandas cannot find enough food to eat.

Plenty of people

China has the largest number of people of any country on Earth—over one billion! To make space for families to build homes, people **clear-cut** forests, or cut down large areas of trees. Bamboo is cut down, as well. People use it as material for making clothing, paper, and for building homes. Bamboo also feeds people and **livestock**. Each area of bamboo that is cut down shrinks panda habitats.

Bamboo die-backs

Bamboo forests flower and make new plants only about once every 20 to 100 years. After flowering, all the bamboo plants in an area die. This event is called a **bamboo die-back**. Large areas of bamboo can die back at the same time. After a die-back, it can take five years for new bamboo plants to grow.

Where to go?

When bamboo die-backs occurred in the past, pandas simply moved to new home ranges with living bamboo. Today, many bamboo forests are separated by farms and highways that pandas cannot safely cross. When pandas are unable to reach new patches of bamboo, they starve.

Poaching pandas

Some people hunt and kill pandas. Pandas are often killed for their fur. People around the world pay a lot of money for panda fur. Panda fur is made into rugs and wall hangings. In 1962, the Chinese government made it **illegal**, or against the law, for people to hunt pandas. Many pandas are still killed by **poachers**, however. Poachers are people who hunt animals illegally.

Stopping poachers

It is difficult for police to stop poachers. China's forests are very thick, so it is easy for poachers to hide among the trees. Another reason poachers are hard to catch is that there are few people to guard the areas where pandas live.

Poachers set traps for other animals that live in panda home ranges, but pandas often get caught in these traps.

Not enough cubs

The panda **population** is very low. Population is the total number of one type of animal in an area. Part of the reason that there are so few pandas is that pandas do not **reproduce**, or have cubs, often enough to increase their population. A female panda is not able to mate until she is five or six years old. When she is ready to mate, there may not be a male panda nearby with whom she can mate. If there is not a male nearby, the female will not be able to mate that year. When a female panda does have a cub, she stops mating until her cub has left to find its own home range. Most female pandas have only seven or eight cubs in their lifetimes.

24

Panda cubs in danger

Panda cubs are almost helpless, and even their mothers cannot protect them all the time. Many cubs do not become adults because they are eaten by predators such as leopards, foxes, and wild dogs. These cubs never get a chance to have their own babies.

Many young pandas are eaten by wild dogs.

Inbreeding

Each year, panda habitats become smaller and farther away from one another. Many pandas have trouble finding new mating partners, so they mate with closely related partners year after year. Mating with related pandas is called **inbreeding**. Inbred pandas catch diseases more easily and find it more difficult to have cubs of their own.

In order to have healthy babies, pandas must be able to travel to areas where other pandas live.

Protecting pandas

China is home to all the wild pandas of the world. The Chinese government has been working for many years to help save pandas. In 1979, the government teamed up with WWF to find new ways to protect panda habitats. Today, there are 40 panda **preserves** in China. A preserve is a large area of land that is protected by a government. Cutting down bamboo plants or trees on a panda preserve is against the law. This law protects the dense forests and bamboo plants that pandas need to survive.

Underground tunnels

In Sichuan, highways or villages separate sections of panda habitats. People are now helping to build tunnels under, and passages across, these areas. Pandas can use the tunnels and passages to find food in new areas during bamboo die-backs. They can also use them to find other pandas during **mating season**.

Learning lessons

Preserves have **research centers** where scientists study pandas to learn more about these animals and their behaviors. Research centers are also safe places where pandas can mate and give birth to cubs. As scientists learn more about pandas, they may also discover how to protect these animals and their habitats.

Pandemonium!

*Pandas can live to be 30 years old in **captivity**, or under human care.*

When pandas were first taken from China to live in zoos around the world, visitors to the zoos became very excited! The word "pandemonium" means "a very noisy place." It was used to describe how excited people were about seeing giant pandas.

A panda present

Pandas that live in zoos outside China are usually gifts from the Chinese government to the zoos. Receiving a panda as a gift is an honor for any zoo. It is also a great responsibility. The zoo must provide the panda with a safe and healthy home.

Home sweet home!

Over the past twenty years, zoos have greatly improved the living conditions of pandas. In the past, pandas were often fed different kinds of fruits, vegetables, or even **pellets**. Today, pandas in zoos are almost always fed bamboo. They are given large areas in which to live and explore. Zoos provide water pools for drinking and playing, trees for climbing, and rocks on which pandas can make scent markings. In places with hot summers, zoos provide pandas with air-conditioned areas, so they can escape the heat.

Pandas are safe in zoos. They grow up to be healthy and playful, but their lives are not the same as the lives of pandas in the wild.

Help a panda!

Pandas need your help to survive! The best way for you to save these beautiful animals is to help other people learn about them and why they are endangered. A fun way to teach others about pandas is to make trivia cards that have panda questions and answers on them.

Use facts from this book and other sources to create questions about pandas. Ask your friends and family to do some reading about pandas and then use your trivia cards to test their knowledge!

Here is a fun fact to use on one of your trivia cards: Pandas eat for twelve to fourteen hours a day!

So much to know!

You have only begun to learn about giant pandas. There are many other facts waiting to be discovered in magazines, videos, and books at your local library. Another great place to learn about pandas is on the Internet. To get started, visit these websites:

• **www.panda.org**

This website is home to the WWF. Learn all about pandas, as well as hundreds of other endangered animals!

• **www.sandiegozoo.org**

The San Diego Zoo allows you to watch a panda live on video! Visit their website and click on "panda cam."

Glossary

Note: Boldfaced words that are defined in the text may not appear in the glossary.

backbone A set of bones that runs down the middle of an animal's back

captivity A state of being in an enclosed area such as a zoo

landslide An event caused by soil and rocks sliding down a hill or mountain

livestock Animals such as cattle that are raised by people for food

logo A name or symbol that is easy to recognize

mating season The time of year during which pandas mate

mountainous Describing an area that is covered by mountains

pellet A small, solid ball of food

pith A soft, spongy substance found inside the center of a plant's stem

scent gland The part of a panda's bottom that produces a strong-smelling substance used to mark its home range

scent marking An odor left by a panda to mark its territory and warn others to stay away

stalk The main part of a plant that is soft and not woody

Index

bamboo 7, 8, 11, 13, 14, 15, 18-19, 20, 21, 26, 27, 29
China 7, 8, 20, 22, 26, 28
communication 17
cubs 13, 14, 15, 24, 25, 27
dens 9, 13, 14
endangered 4-5, 7, 30, 31
food 8, 11, 14, 18, 20, 27
forests 6, 8, 9, 15, 20, 21, 22, 26

fur 6, 10, 13, 15, 22
habitat loss 20
habitats 8, 20, 25, 26, 27
home ranges 9, 16, 21, 22, 24
how to help 30-31
life cycle 12-13
mammals 6, 12
mating 12, 13, 16, 17, 24, 25, 27

mountains 8, 9, 20
paws 11, 17, 19
poachers 22
population 24
predators 14, 15, 25
preserves 26-27
red pandas 7
scent markings 16, 29
territories 9, 16
zoos 28-29

1 2 3 4 5 6 7 8 9 0   Printed in the U.S.A. 4 3 2 1 0 9 8 7 6 5